FOCUS ON
MAMMALS

Jane Parker

SHOOTING STAR PRESS®

This edition produced in **1995** for
Shooting Star Press Inc
Suite 1212, 230 Fifth Avenue
New York, NY 10001

© Aladdin Books Ltd 1995

Created and produced by
Aladdin Books Ltd
28 Percy Street
London W1P 0LD

*First published in
the United States in 1995 by*
Shooting Star Press Inc

ISBN 1-57335-325-6

Editor	Selina Wood
Design	David West Children's Book Design
Designer	Ed Simkins
Series Director	Bibby Whittaker
Illustrator	Dave Burroughs
Picture research	Brooks Krikler Research

*The author, Jane Parker, has a degree in
zoology, and has worked as a researcher at
London Zoo. She now works as a writer,
researcher and indexer.*

*The consultant, Joyce Pope, was a senior
lecturer at the Natural History Museum. She
now writes, lectures, and keeps and studies
many types of mammals.*

INTRODUCTION

Many of the animals which are most familiar to us, such as dogs and horses, are mammals. As members of this family, we share with them certain characteristics, such as keen senses and an instinct to care for offspring, which set us all apart from other animal groups. This book reveals the fascinating world of mammals, from the mighty blue whale to the pygmy shrew. It describes how mammals have adapted to every habitat, how they hunt and hide, and court and communicate. The book traces the age-old relationship between people and other mammals, with information on the arts, language and literature, science and math, history, and geography. The key below shows how subjects are divided.

Geography
The symbol of the planet Earth indicates where there is geographical information in the book. One of these sections describes the seasonal whale migration from the equator to the Arctic and back.

Language and Literature
An open book is the sign for activities and information which involve language and literature. This includes a look at the many stories that have been inspired by the world of mammals, including the myth of the Unicorn.

Science and technology
The microscope symbol indicates information about science and technology. It includes a section explaining the different forms and functions of mammal skin and hair.

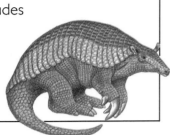

History
The sign of the scroll and hourglass indicates historical information. These sections show how mammals have been valued and cultivated through the ages. Some mammals, such as the cat, have been worshipped as gods.

Math
Information related to mathematics is indicated by the symbol of the ruler, protractor, and compasses. Among topics discussed are the relative speeds of predator and prey.

Arts, crafts, and music
The symbol showing a sheet of music and art tools indicates arts, crafts, or musical information. It examines the way that mammals are portrayed in films and cartoons.

CONTENTS

WHAT ARE MAMMALS?

Mammals are the most successful animals with backbones on Earth today. There are about 4,500 species, and they live in all habitats, from the coldest to the hottest, on land, in the sea, and in the air. Each one looks different, but in certain ways they are all alike. Mammals have large brains and keen senses. They communicate by sounds, smells, and visual means. They are warm-blooded, have an efficient circulation system and they care for their young. Human beings can even change their environment.

Mother's Milk

One of the reasons for the success of mammals is the care that they give to their young. Mothers provide instant food until the babies are big enough to feed themselves. This food, a liquid secretion called *milk*, contains nutrients and immunity to some diseases. It is made by mammary glands under the mother's skin, and the baby sucks it from nipples during nursing.

First Mammals

The last 65 million years, since the dinosaurs died out, has been the "Age of Mammals." But the first mammals appeared long before this, about 200 million years ago. They evolved from a group of mammal-like reptiles that were successful even before the reign of the dinosaurs. *Megazostrodon* and *Purgatorius* were among the first true mammals. These tiny animals hid in trees and undergrowth, hunting insects at night.

Taeniolabis
(An early plant eater)

Purgatorius

Megazostrodon

Warm Blood

Mammals can live in any climate because they are warm-blooded, or *endothermic*. This means they can keep their bodies at the same temperature no matter how cold or hot the weather is. Endotherms generate heat by chemical reactions that go on inside the body tissues. They keep this heat in with layers of insulating fat and fur. If they get too hot, most mammals can produce sweat. Sweat is a liquid secreted onto the skin surface which evaporates and cools the body.

Food, Clothes, and Shelter

When people migrated from the warmth of Africa, where they first evolved, to colder northern latitudes, they began to use the skins of other mammals to keep themselves warm. In the far north, where there were no caves and no trees to build huts, they used colossal mammoth bones and tusks for the framework of shelters. This may have led to the first man-made extinctions, about 10,000 years ago, when the mammoths died out.

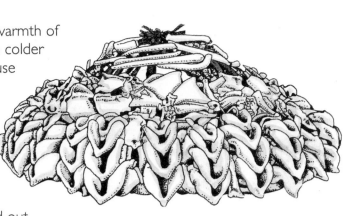

Vertebrates

Mammals belong to the group of animals known as *vertebrates*. They all have backbones as part of their internal skeletons. Skeletons provide support and protection for internal organs and enable movement. A gorilla's skeleton (left) is similar to that of an orang-utan (above).

Aesop's Fables

Aesop was a Greek storyteller who lived in the 6th century B.C. He used animal stories to show people how to deal with life's little problems, and to teach right from wrong. One story (below) tells of a race between a slow tortoise (a reptile) and a swift hare (a mammal). The hare is so far ahead, and so confident of victory, he takes a nap. The tortoise plods

along steadily, passing the hare, who wakes up to see his opponent crossing the finishing line. The tale teaches that persistence can be more important than speed.

Adaptable Mammals

After the demise of the dinosaurs, mammals soon adapted to fill every habitat. Some mammals are perfectly adapted to a particular habitat. Dolphins are so well adjusted to life in the water they can no longer live on land. Others survive by being adaptable. The wolf lives by its wits, eating almost anything it can find, and taking advantage of any situation.

HAIR & FUR

Mammals keep themselves warm with fur or hairs which trap a layer of insulating air. Most have two kinds of fur – a thick layer of soft under-fur, and a thin layer of long guard hairs. Hair is coated with a waterproof substance called sebum which helps keep the animal dry. Hair comes in different colors and patterns which are used for recognition or camouflage, and it must be kept clean. Many mammals use grooming to cement social relationships; hair is sensitive to touch.

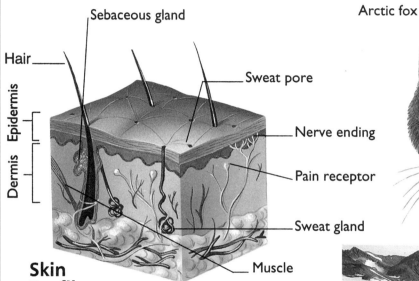

Sebaceous gland

Hair

Epidermis

Dermis

Sweat pore

Nerve ending

Pain receptor

Sweat gland

Muscle

Arctic fox

Skin Profile

Skin is the largest organ of the body. It keeps infections, poisons, and water out. It contains nerves which respond to touch, pain, and heat, and can repair itself when it gets damaged. It is the main temperature-regulating organ. Each hair grows from a tiny hole or follicle, which has a nerve, a muscle, blood vessels, and a sebaceous gland.

Prickles and Scales

Hair is made from a hard substance called keratin. Some mammals have sharp, rigid hairs in their coats. These spines form an excellent protection from predators. Hedgehogs roll up into a prickly ball when threatened, while porcupines turn their backs on their enemy and run — backward! Pangolin hair is modified to form scales. But the armor plating of armadillos is made from bony plates in the skin. When pangolins or armadillos roll themselves up they are safe from attack.

Armadillo

6

Fierce Warriors

In Papua New Guinea the native people often argue over territory. Their battles are usually ceremonial, but they dress up in huge head-dresses (made from fur and feathers), and pierce their skin with echidna spines to look fierce.

The Arctic fox changes its coat from snowy white in winter to rocky brown in summer, making it difficult for predators to see. It also helps it creep up on *its* prey, the Arctic hare.

Spots and Stripes

As Rudyard Kipling says in the *Just So Stories*, giraffe blotches, zebra stripes, and leopard spots are a good disguise when the animals are in the dappled light under trees. But how do zebra stripes work out in the open? Some scientists think they might be an optical illusion which confuses or dazzles predators, making it difficult for them to launch a chase. Others think the stripes help zebras recognize members of their own herd, so they can keep together.

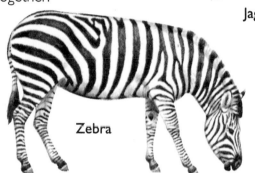

Jaguar

Zebra

Fashionable Furs

In the last century, wearing the furry skins, or pelts, of beautiful mammals became fashionable. Hunting and trapping became big business. Millions of minks, foxes, seals, sea otters, and sables were killed and many, as a result, are close to extinction. Today many people object to killing animals for the sake of fashion (left), and campaign against the fur trade.

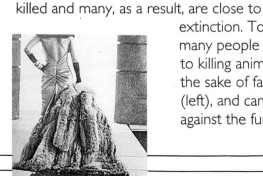

Let your hair down!

Rapunzel was a beautiful young girl who had been locked in a tower by a wicked witch. During her captive years the girl's hair had grown to an extraordinary length. Every day the witch climbed up the thick plait of hair with food. Then a handsome prince came by and used the same trick to rescue Rapunzel. They lived happily ever after, but could this story be true? Human hair is stronger than steel fibers and the record for the longest hair is 13 feet, 6 inches. But hair this length is usually very brittle.

COURTSHIP & BREEDING

Mammals have elaborate courtship rituals, to ensure that they choose the healthiest and strongest mate. They also maintain territories, by fighting off intruders, in order to provide enough food for the babies. Mammals have highly developed senses of smell, hearing, and vision, which are used during courtship rituals and territorial disputes. Some leave scents, some howl and others perform displays. Hares (below) twist and jump in the air.

Courtship

Courtship rituals prepare the way for mating. They ensure both animals belong to the same species, are the right sex and are healthy. Most male mammals prove how fit they are by fighting. Usually these fights are just "show" to avoid too much bloodshed. Stallions (male horses) fight with their teeth and hooves, but the long mane gives some protection. Stags (male deer) fight using their antlers and have thick neck fat to absorb the blows. The season when stags fight is called the rut. The winner is the strongest and can mate with the females.

Courtship also gets animals in the right mood for mating, reduces fear and aggression, and allows close contact. Wolves use scents, body postures, and growls and whines during courtship.

Too Many Lemmings

When there is abundant vegetation under the Arctic snow, mother lemmings have several litters with up to 10 babies. The population increases sharply. But every four years or so the food runs out and they set off on migration. In the panic many are killed and the numbers return to normal.

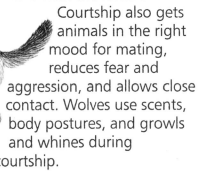

Monogamy

Most mammal breeding systems are polygamous, i.e. one male mates with several females, like lions (left). The male may live with his harem of females, helping to rear the young, or he may take no part in family life. Only a few mammals, like gibbons, dik-diks, beavers (right), and elephant shrews are monogamous; one male and one female stay together all their lives forming a stable family unit.

Birthday

A baby mammal develops inside its mother's womb or uterus. The baby's blood vessels pass along a tube called the *umbilical cord* and into an organ called the *placenta*. They pass close to the mother's blood vessels and pick up food and oxygen. At first, the baby is called an embryo, but as it grows bigger it becomes a fetus. Before birth the mother often makes a nest to keep the babies warm. Birth occurs at the end of the pregnancy, or gestation period, when the womb muscles contract to push the babies out. The mother licks each baby to break membranes that surrounded them in the womb. Then she helps them to find the nipple for their first drink of milk, and a strong bond is formed.

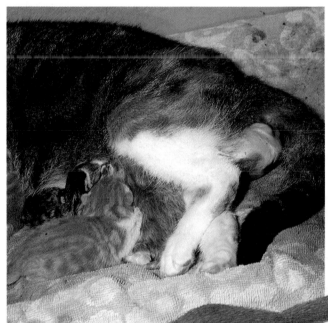

Reproduction

Most other vertebrates – reptiles, amphibians, fish, and birds – lay eggs. Very few give birth to live babies like mammals. The three main groups of mammals have different methods of reproduction.

Monotremes

The platypus and two species of echidna are left-overs from early mammal evolution. They are furry and warm-blooded, but they lay leathery shelled eggs.

Placentals

The largest mammal group keep their young within their womb until they are well developed. The baby's blood picks up food and oxygen through the placenta.

Marsupials

The babies of the kangaroo, wombat and koala are born after a short period of development in the mother's womb. The tiny embryos crawl from the birth canal to their mother's pouch, and attach themselves to a nipple, where they feed and grow.

BABY MAMMALS

Young mammals do not have to fend for themselves until they are almost fully grown. Some, like mice, are born with their eyes closed, have no fur and are cared for in a cosy nest. Others, like zebra foals, are able to run with their mothers very soon after birth. All mammal babies, however, are fed on milk. Mothers, and sometimes fathers, keep their babies clean and warm, teach them the skills they will need in adult life, and protect them from predators. Baby mammals spend a lot of time playing, which strengthens their bodies and improves their co-ordination.

Multi-birth

Wolves grow up in large families. This mother wolf suckles four cubs. She provides shelter in a den and the rest of the adult pack protect them. Babies brought up in dens or nests are happy to be left alone while the mother goes out to search for food. She cannot take them with her until they are much bigger and stronger.

Number of Babies

Having lots of babies at a time is an insurance policy. Parents divide their energy between all the babies in the hope that at least one of them will survive attacks from predators (below). Having only one baby at a time is too risky; if the baby dies the parents have wasted all their energy.

Only Child

The mother sloth hangs upside down and carries her single infant on her stomach. This way she does not need to leave it alone in a den and can protect it all the time. The baby suckles for about one month, but stays put for another five months, reaching out to grab leaves as its mother slowly creeps along the branches. Eventually, it slowly wanders off on its own.

Baby Face

All parents find their babies attractive. This ensures that they will care for their young. The features of all baby mammals are similar – huge eyes set in round faces. These features often appeal to cartoonists and animators. The film *Watership Down*, about a rabbit warren endangered by human destruction, stars young rabbits who have appealing features and individual personalities.

Growth Rates

The rate at which a baby animal grows depends partly on its size. A harvest mouse is independent at 16 days – a giraffe grows for ten years. A gorilla baby also takes ten years to grow. It is much smaller than a giraffe, but it has a much bigger brain. The fastest growth rate of any baby mammal is that of the baby blue whale. During the last two months of pregnancy it puts on 220 pounds of weight daily.

The simplest family is a mother and her babies. In some cases a father is present. Elephants form stable families where babies are looked after by sisters and aunts. The leader is an old female called the *matriarch*.

Meet the family...

1. Sire Bull

2. Matriarch

3. Sisters and Aunts

4. Infant

TO EAT OR BE EATEN

Between them, mammals feed on almost all available foods. Carnivores eat meat, lions are cunning hunters, while hyenas are scavengers. Insectivores, like most bats, specialize in catching tiny insects. Giraffes and rabbits are herbivores – they feed on vegetation. Omnivores, like bears and rats, will eat anything they come across. Mammals use their keen senses and large brains, both to find their food, and to avoid becoming food for others.

Claws and Jaws

Meat is a highly nutritious and easily digested food. Carnivorous mammals have sharp claws on the ends of their toes to help them catch prey. The claws of foxes and polecats sharpen automatically as they wear down. Cats sharpen and clean their claws by dragging them down a tree trunk. They protect them by retracting them into sheaths. Carnivores also have specialized teeth; biting incisors, tearing canines, and crunching premolars and molars.

Insect Eaters

South American anteaters and armadillos open ant and termite nests and scoop up the insects with long, sticky tongues. The unrelated African aardvarks (above) have similar habits.

Animal Speeds

Predator and prey are always well matched. The cheetah is the fastest of all land animals, reaching speeds of 60 miles per hour. But it can only sustain these speeds for short sprints. The gazelles that it chases are not as fast, but they can keep going for a longer time and can swerve easily.

Culling Deer

Wild deer herds have been managed in protected woods and parks for hundreds of years. Today their natural predators, wolves, and bears, have disappeared so the deer are culled to keep their numbers down. Rangers try to mimic a natural predator by shooting the weakest animals and allowing the fittest to live.

Plant Eaters

Plants are not hard to find and do not run away, but they are less nutritious than meat and are difficult to digest. Herbivores who have to eat large quantities of food, need strong grinding teeth and long digestive systems.

Buried Treasure

Hamsters are famous for their habit of hiding food in a secret store in preparation for hard times ahead. They stuff seeds into elastic cheek pouches and carry them back to the burrow. They are not the only mammals that have secret hoards. Leopards often hide their kills in the fork of a tree where they can eat it at leisure. Squirrels bury acorns everywhere so they can retrieve them in winter. Foxes bury bones as do dogs, and moles paralyze earthworms, storing them in their tunnels.

The Masai

The Masai people of East Africa are nomadic cattle-herders who cling to their traditional ways. Their cows are very important. They are used for trade as well as food. The Masai make a sort of black pudding by coagulating milk and blood taken from a vein in a living cow's neck. This diet is supplemented with vegetables.

SMALL MAMMALS

Most mammals are quite small. The most successful mammal group, with more species than any other, is the rodent group. Rodents are intelligent, adaptable animals with high reproductive rates. One quarter of all mammal species are bats. The smallest mammal of all is the tiny Kitti's hog-nosed bat which weighs only $1/20$ oz. The earliest placentals were insectivores. They are secretive night-time or underground animals.

Rodents and Insectivores

Beavers, squirrels, gophers, mice, rats, voles, hamsters, dormice, porcupines, guinea pigs, and mole-rats are all rodents. They are opportunists who make the most of whatever is available. They are found in every habitat, from lemmings under the Arctic snow to gerbils in the parched desert. Rabbits are not rodents, but are closely related. Long-snouted tenrecs, moles, shrews, and hedgehogs are insectivores.

Rats!

Bubonic plague is caused by a bacterium that infects rat fleas. People get the plague from flea bites and spread the disease when they sneeze. Infected people suffer fever and swollen lymph nodes (called buboes) and soon die. Epidemics have killed millions of people. In the 14th century, belongings were burned in an attempt to control the disease.

A Winter's Tale

When the weather is very cold the dormouse hibernates. First it eats large amounts of food and gets fat, then it curls up in its cosy nest. Its temperature drops to just above freezing, and its heart beat and breathing almost stop. In this state the dormouse uses very little energy and it can survive the winter.

Bats

Bats are the only mammals that can truly fly. Bat wings are formed from skin stretched over extended arm and hand bones. Most bats are nocturnal, and hide away by day in roosts. They feed on flying insects which they find in the dark. They make very high-pitched squeaks, that humans cannot hear. They can work out where the insect is from the time it takes the echo of the squeak to return, after bouncing off the insect.

Nocturnal Animals

Many small mammals are nocturnal. They come out only at night when predators that hunt by sight cannot see well. They also avoid competition with daytime animals that feed on the same food. In very hot, dry places, animals like gerbils stay hidden in dark, damp burrows in the day, coming out only at night when it is cool. Nocturnal animals, such as the urban fox (right), have well-developed senses of smell or touch to find their way around.

Animal Sizes

The African elephant stands 13 feet high and weighs six tons. Its heart beats 25 times a minute to pump enough blood for its ponderous movements. The pygmy shrew is only two inches long and weighs just two grams. It hardly ever stops scampering about and its tiny heart beats over 800 times every minute.

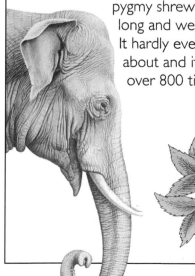

Wind in the Willows

These charming stories about the antics of the small mammalian friends Mole, Water Rat, Badger, and the rather pompous but loveable amphibian, Toad of Toad Hall, were first written by Kenneth Grahame as a series of bedtime stories for his son Alastair. The full collection of stories, called *The Wind in the Willows*, was published in 1908.

HOOVES ON THE MOVE

Hoofed animals, or *ungulates*, walk on the tips of their toes which are protected by hard hooves. Hooves are made from keratin, the same horny material as claws and nails. Solid hooves are an adaptation for running away from predators. Ungulates are divided into three groups: the elephants and their relatives (such as hyraxes); the perissodactyls or odd-toed ungulates, such as horses and zebras; and the artiodactyls or even-toed ungulates, such as cattle.

Odds and Evens

The skeletons of ungulate feet show how they walk on the tips of their toes. Originally all mammals had five digits or toes. But as ungulates evolved they lost toes to improve their speed. Some ungulates, like elephants, still have five toes. Pig trotters have two large hooves and two small hooves which do not touch the ground. Rhinos (upper left) walk on three toes, deer have four (lower left) but walk upon two, and horses have only one.

Diseases

Foot-and-mouth disease affects animals with cloven (split) hooves, such as cattle and sheep. It spreads rapidly through the herds and can bankrupt farmers. Some animal diseases spread to humans. Sleeping sickness is transferred from cattle to humans via the blood-sucking tsetse fly (below).

Mythical Horses

In Ancient Greek mythology, the winged Pegasus flew up to heaven and was tamed by the goddess Athena with a magical golden bridle. The Unicorn is a white horse with a spiral horn growing from its forehead. It is said that whoever drinks from its horn is protected from poisoning.

Migration

Many animals make seasonal migrations to new habitats, to find better living conditions. Huge herds of wildebeest walk hundreds of miles across the African plains in search of grass and water. The urge to move is so strong they will tackle any obstacle. Many die on the way, drowning in rivers, falling down gorges, or caught by predators.

Ungulate Relatives

Camels (left) and llamas are even-toed ungulates. But they do not walk on the tips of their toes like other cloven-hoofed animals. The weight is carried by soft pads behind their hooves. Camels are ideally suited for desert life. Their wide feet do not sink in the sand, their humps store food for long-distance travel, and their stomachs can hold 22 gallons of water. Rhinos are primitive relatives of horses. They have stumpy feet with three hoofed toes, and thick, hairless skin folded into armorlike plates.

Horsemanship

Man's first association with horses was to hunt them for meat. Horses were domesticated in Asia about 6,000 years ago. Until the horse collar was invented, horses were not used to pull heavy loads, but for pulling warriors in chariots. In the Middle Ages horses were bred to be strong enough to carry knights in full armor. These thoroughbreds are among the 150 breeds known today.

Zebras (left) are closely related to horses and donkeys. They live in sociable groups, grazing on the African plains.

THE GREAT GRAZERS

Being very large, like elephants, rhinos, and hippos, has its advantages. Large animals have lower metabolic rates than smaller animals – they move more slowly, have slower heartbeats, do not loose heat quickly and live longer. Large herbivores can survive on poorer quality food than small ones, feeding on wood and roots that are available all year. They can defend themselves by their sheer size and do not need to be fast runners. They have pillar-like legs rather than the long, slender limbs of smaller ungulates.

Working Elephants

Elephants are strong, sociable and intelligent and have powerful memories. These characteristics make them easy to train for riding and moving heavy objects like logs. They have worked for people for over 5,000 years, but they do not breed easily in captivity and are not truly domesticated. The smaller Asian elephant is still used today in the lumber industry, and for ceremonial parades and circuses. But the larger African elephant, once used by Hannibal in battle, is not so reliable and now rarely works.

Rhinos

Rhinos are bad-tempered and nearsighted herbivores, who defend territories by threatening intruders with their horns. Despite stumpy legs and heavy bodies they can charge at surprising speed. Some prefer to feed on grass (right). Other species have prehensile (grasping) lips. to get at foliage on trees, which they can push over!

Underwater Grazers

Dugongs and manatees, the Sirenians, are the only mammalian underwater grazers. Sirenians come to the water's surface only to breathe. They probably evolved from the same ancestors as the ungulates. When their front teeth get worn by tough water weeds they fall out and are replaced by new ones at the back. Elephants have the same system of tooth renewal.

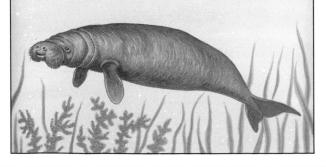

Ungulate Digestion

Herbivores use bacteria to break down indigestible plant material. They have evolved two ways of doing this. Tapirs (left), elephants, rhinos, and horses, are hindgut fermenters. The food is broken down by enzymes as it passes along the digestive tract to the *caecum*, a chamber where the fermenting (digesting) bacteria get to work. Cattle, sheep, deer, camels, and giraffes are ruminants. They regurgitate food and "chew the cud." Then they swallow it again and it is fermented in a second stomach called the rumen.

Conservation

Despite a world-wide ban on trade in ivory and powdered rhino horn, poachers still make money by killing elephants and rhinos. Many Asian people believe that the powered horn of the rhinoceros has magical powers. Competition from farmers, who are associated with habitat destruction, has severely reduced elephant populations in Africa, and three of the world's five rhino species are also very close to extinction.

Versatile Trunk

The elephant's trunk is a muscular extension of the nose and upper lip. It is used for breathing, smelling, picking up food, spraying water, caressing, and amplifying the rumbles which elephants make to communicate.

Rhino horns are sawn off without harming the animal, to prevent it from being murdered by poachers (above). This practice has actually increased the rhino population. Elephant tusks are burned (left), to stop them being sold illegally.

CATS

The cat family, the Felidae, are all very similar in shape though they come in different sizes. They are all agile hunters that stalk and pounce on their prey. They have excellent stereoscopic vision, they can see in color and in the dark. They have a special layer at the back of the eye, called the tapetum, which reflects light back to the retina, so they can see in low light. All cats have sensitive whiskers for night-time hunting.

Small Cats

There are 28 species of "small cats." Apart from their size they are very similar to big cats. Small cats can purr, but they cannot roar. Big cats can roar, but cannot purr. The domestic cat (bottom), is descended from the wild cat, which was found in Europe and North Africa. The bobcat, and the lynx (top), are peculiar in having ear tufts and short tails. Many small cats, like the ocelot, have spotted coats for camouflage in the forest.

Cheshire Cat

The grinning Cheshire cat, in *Alice's Adventures in Wonderland*, by Lewis Carroll, caused some difficulty when the Queen of Hearts ordered "Off with its head." The Cheshire cat was able to make its body invisible. The executioner was puzzled as to how he could cut a head off a body that was not there. While the king debated the matter the queen threatened to have all the court executed. Meanwhile the cat had disappeared!

Witch's Cats

Cats have lived alongside people for some 5,000 years, ridding homes of mice and rats. But in the Middle Ages they became associated with witchcraft and the devil. They were cruelly persecuted along with their owners. The Christian Church also tried to rid the world of them because they were symbols of paganism.

Record Breakers

The cheetah is the fastest land animal in the world. It can reach speeds of 60 miles per hour. It can move so fast because it stores energy in its springlike backbone. When it runs its backbone alternately stretches and coils, swinging its long legs forward and backward.

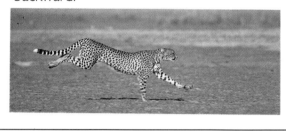

Big Cats

Tigers, cheetahs, leopards, and jaguars are solitary hunters. They usually stalk medium-sized grazers no bigger than themselves. Lions take larger prey, and hunt in prides. Prides consist of a full-grown male and several breeding females and their cubs. Big cats hunt only when they are hungry, gorging on the kill and then dozing for several days.

Tiger Jaguar

Lion

Agility

Cats are supposed to have "nine lives" – they almost always land on their feet. They do this by a reflex action controlled by the organ of balance in the inner ear. It tells the brain which way up the cat is. The brain matches this information with messages from the eyes. The neck muscles turn the head to the upright position and the body follows – all before the cat hits the ground. Cats are agile climbers, clinging on with their claws. They have powerful legs and can spring straight up into the air, landing on their prey on all fours.

DOGS

The dog family, or Canidae, includes dogs, wolves, jackals, and foxes. Dogs tend to take advantage of any situation, feeding on carrion, insects, and even fruit and leaves, if they cannot hunt. They can all run at speed for long distances, but are less agile than cats. Dogs are intelligent, sociable animals and most live as tightly-knit family groups or packs, at least for part of the year. They communicate by sounds, body postures, and their highly developed sense of smell.

Domestic Dogs

The earliest remains of a domestic dog are believed to be over 11,000 years old. Abandoned wolf pups may have been taken into the home as pets, guard dogs, or hunters. Dogs treat the families they live with as members of their pack, taking their place in the hierarchy. As with other domestic animals, many different breeds have been produced, each with different characteristics.

Big Bad Wolf

Wolves have had a bad image for centuries because they kill domestic animals and game if they have to. There are many stories, but few proven cases, of attacks on people. Fairy stories about the Big Bad Wolf and legends of werewolves (right) reflect the fear of wolves. It has lead to centuries of persecution. Today the gray wolf, which once roamed most of the northern hemisphere, is an endangered animal. Efforts to re-introduce it involve improving its image.

Hot and Cold Foxes

The Arctic fox, as its name suggests, lives in the cold Arctic tundra. It can survive temperatures as low as -50°C. It has a coat of thick fur all over its body, even on the pads of its paws, and on its small, rounded ears. They are so well insulated that they loose very little heat.

Pavlov

Ivan Pavlov was a Russian doctor who spent a lot of time finding out how the human body works. He used dogs for his experiments. He discovered he could train them to salivate with a bell, not just in response to food. When the body learns to perform a function in response to an artificial cue it is called a conditioned reflex.

Peter and the Wolf

The Russian composer Prokofiev wrote this musical fairy tale for children in 1936. The story is told by a narrator and all the characters – Peter, his grandfather, the wolf, the bird, the cat, and the duck – are played by different musical instruments from the orchestra. The wolf is portrayed by three horns.

Wolf

Coyote

Jackal

Canine Relatives

The closest relatives of the domestic dog are wolves, coyotes, and jackals. Members of a wolf pack hunt together co-operatively to bring down large prey. The North American coyote is one of the few wild animals that is increasing in numbers today. An adaptable animal, it eats anything it can find. A breeding pair of African jackals stay mated for life.

Working Dogs

Many domestic dogs work for their living, helping on the farm or with field sports, racing and guarding or guiding their owners. Huskies, bred for their strength and resilience, work together in teams, pulling sledges across the snow.

The tiny Fennec fox, the smallest of all the wild dogs, lives in hot African deserts. It keeps itself cool by sleeping in a burrow during the hottest part of the day. It uses its huge ears as radiators to get rid of excess body heat. They are also useful for listening to the sounds of the tiny animals on which it feeds.

FINS & FLIPPERS

Many mammals have adapted successfully to living in water, feeding on fish, shellfish, or plankton. Water mammals are smooth and streamlined with paddle or flipper-shaped limbs and thick layers of fat or fur for insulation. All underwater mammals must come to the surface regularly to breathe, but seals and whales can dive to great depths in search of food, staying down for long periods of time. Seals and otters can move on land, but whales never leave the water.

Toothed...
Most fish eaters, like otters, seals, or killer whales, have sharp, peg-like teeth to grip slippery fish they feed upon. Shellfish require a tougher approach. Walruses prize them off the bottom with long canine teeth or tusks. Sea otters smash shells with a stone.

...Or Toothless
The largest of all animals, the baleen whales, have no teeth. They feed on the tiny floating creatures of the plankton, filtering them from the water through huge combs of baleen or "whalebone" in their mouths.

Platypus
The strange platypus looks at first like an otter with a duck's bill. It digs burrows in Australian river banks where it lays its eggs (see page 9). Platypuses swim well under the water with their webbed feet, delving in the mud for tiny creatures with their sensitive bills.

Beaver
Beavers are rodents that can gnaw through tree trunks. They dam forest streams with the felled trees to make deep pools. Here they build lodges with underwater entrances where they can raise their young in safety. They feed on twigs and bark from logs stored under the water.

Babies
Seals, sealions, otters, and beavers go on land to give birth, where the babies stay until they can swim. But whales, dugongs and manatees cannot leave the water and so have underwater births. The babies are well developed when born. Sea otters also have their young in the water. They float on their backs, carrying their young on their stomachs.

Mermaids
Mermaids are legendary sea creatures, beautiful women with fish tails instead of legs. Sailors who "saw" them thought they foretold disaster. In Greek mythology, the Sirens sang beautiful songs to lure sailors onto the rocks. They had women's heads and the bodies of birds. These creatures might well have been manatees or seals seen from a distance.

Whale Trail
Humpback whales perform long migration journeys. They spend the winter in warm coastal waters near the equator where the babies are born. In the spring the whales set off for the Arctic or Antarctic, a journey of many thousands of miles. Here the cool currents are rich in the plankton and tiny shrimps that the whales feed upon.

Red arrows = summer migration

Blue arrows = winter migration

Dolphin
Dolphins and porpoises are toothed whales. They are very intelligent and sociable creatures. They find and stun fish by sonar, a sort of underwater echolocation. The largest dolphin is the killer whale.

Manatee
Manatees and dugongs have lost their back limbs and replaced them with a flat, gristly tail fluke. Their front legs have become flippers.

Whale
Whales breathe through a blowhole on the top of their heads. They hold their breath underwater and breathe out a fountain of exhaled air, mucus, and water vapor, at the surface.

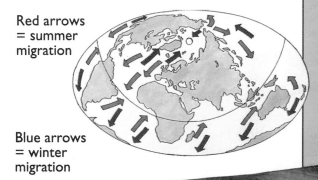

LIFE IN THE TREES

Living in trees provides a ready source of insects, fruits, leaves, and flowers for food. Trees also provide protection from ground-dwelling predators. Many unrelated mammals like squirrels, pangolins, sloths, and koalas live in trees. But perhaps the most accomplished tree dwellers are primates, the monkeys and their relatives, apes. Tree-dwellers need large brains to co-ordinate their well-developed senses of vision and balance, and a strong and sensitive grip.

Lemur

Tarsier

Tree shrew

Lower Primates
Some scientists consider tree shrews and flying lemurs to be primitive primates. But the prosimians – lemurs, lorises, bushbabies, pottos, and tarsiers – are definitely related to monkeys. They have smaller brains, longer noses and a better-developed sense of smell than their higher primate cousins.

Old World, New World
Monkeys are divided into two groups. Those that live in the Old World (Africa, Asia, and Indonesia) are called catarrhine (downward-nosed) monkeys. They include the baboons, macaques, mandrills, mangabeys, and colobus monkeys. The tiny marmosets and tamarins and larger capuchin monkeys live in the New World (the Americas). They are called platyrrhine (wide-nosed) monkeys.

Capuchin

Colobus

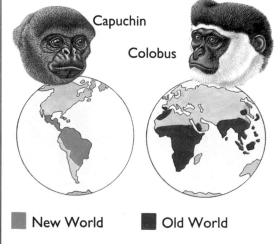

■ New World   ■ Old World

Medicine Monkeys

Human beings are primates, so scientists use monkeys to study human biology and diseases. Rhesus monkeys, from Asia, are noted for their usefulness in medical research. Studies of their blood, in 1940, revealed a new blood group, the Rh factor – a discovery which enabled safer blood transfusions to be given.

Hands and Feet

Primate hands and feet are adapted for climbing. They have long, flexible fingers and toes, with "thumbs" that can grip right round the branches. The ends of the fingers and toes form sensitive pads with flat nails, instead of claws. These features have produced the dextrous human hand.

Chimp

Higher Primates

Monkeys, lesser apes, and great apes are called simians. The spider monkey from the New World has a prehensile tail which it uses as a fifth limb. Gibbons are lesser apes. They spend a lot of time swinging through the trees using their arms. Chimps, gorillas, orangutans, and humans are great apes. They are less agile and spend more time on the ground.

Gibbon

Spider Monkey

King Kong

King Kong was the star of early horror films. He was a giant gorilla, discovered in the jungle and brought back to the US to be put on display. But the "giant", who could hold a woman in the palm of his hand, was only a model 20 inches tall. His jointed limbs were moved a little at a time, between film frames.

MAMMALS & PEOPLE

Throughout our history we have relied heavily on other mammals for many of our needs. Ever since we began to supplement our vegetarian diet by hunting, we have used their flesh and, later, milk for food; their skins and fur for clothes; their bones and horns for tools and weapons; their strength for transport and their trust for companionship. Unfortunately, we have often repaid them by persecution to the point of extinction. It is time for us to help them survive.

Food

We Need Mammals

Mammals provide: meat and milk – highly nutritious foods, rich in proteins, fats and minerals. Mammal furs or pelts keep people warm in cold climates. Leather is used for working clothes and saddlery. Wool is clipped hair, spun into strands and woven or knitted into garments. Horses, oxen, elephants, and camels are used to carry or pull people or their possessions, to plough the fields or to make war on others. Mammals are used by scientists to investigate diseases and drugs, and even space travel.

Clothing

Transport

Science

Religion

Many of the world's religions reflect the close links between people and mammals. The ancient Egyptians worshipped hundreds of gods, who were involved in every aspect of daily life. The cat goddess, Bast, was responsible for contentment and warmth. Her worship involved singing and dancing. The monkey-headed god, Hanuman, is a Hindu god. He is clever, skillful, and loyal. He helped to rescue Sita, the wife of the god Rama, when she was abducted from India to Sri Lanka.

Working Mammals

Oxen are still used for draft work in developing countries, pulling ploughs and wagons. Their strength helps to feed people. Guide dogs work for blind people. They are especially trained to lead their owners around obstacles in their path. Police rely on the dog's sensitive nose to find criminals and sniff out drugs.

Pets

Pets can give great pleasure and relief from stress. Cats, dogs, horses, even hamsters can form strong bonds with owners. But we must remember that pets are dependent on us for all their needs.

Extinctions

Extinctions caused by humans began when Ice Age people discovered how to kill mammoths and woolly rhinos with weapons. The rate has increased dramatically over the last 100 years and now several species are added to the list daily. Despite whaling bans some countries still insist that they need to kill whales for "scientific research". The blue whale's population has shrunk to around 1,400 from an original 250,000.

One Man and his Dog

A young wolf makes friends with a Stone Age youth. Its laid-back ears show that it is willing to accept a subordinate position in the human family pack. The youth crouches to avoid threatening the wolf and makes physical contact. Perhaps this is how man found his best friend; a friendship that has lasted thousands of years.

Noah and his Ark

According to the Bible, Noah was the only God-fearing man of his time. His was chosen by God to keep some people and animals alive during a great flood sent to purge the Earth. Noah filled a huge ark with his family and a male and female from every species of animal. After 40 days and nights of rain, they emerged safely from the ark.

VARIETY OF MAMMALS

MARSUPIALS
(Pouched mammals)
Kangeroo

MONOTREMES
(Egg-laying mammals)
Platypus

EDENTATES
Armadillo

INSECTIVORES
Hedgehog

PRIMATES
Capuchin
monkey

CARNIVORES
Wolf

PANGOLINS
Pangolin

SEALS & SEALIONS
Sealion

AARDVARKS
Aardvark

FLYING LEMURS
Flying lemur

LAGOMORPHS
Rabbit

RODENTS
Rat

WHALES &
DOLPHINS
Sperm whale

BATS
Long-eared bat

EVEN-TOED
UNGULATES
Hippopotamus

HYRAXES
Tree hyrax

ODD-TOED
UNGULATES
Zebra

ELEPHANTS
African elephant

SEA COWS
Manatee

GLOSSARY

Bacteria Tiny single-celled organisms which can only be seen with a microscope.

Blowhole A nostril at the top of a whale's head which is a breathing hole.

Camouflage Patterns, colors and shapes that disguise animals so they cannot be seen by their predators or prey.

Culling The killing of old or sick animals to keep numbers down, so that the remaining healthy animal will have enough food.

Digestive system A long tube passing through an animal where food is broken down by enzymes into smaller and smaller bits until it can pass into the blood stream.

Domesticated animals Animals bred by humans to suit human needs.

Endotherm An animal that uses chemical energy to maintain a constant internal body temperature, no matter what the surrounding temperature.

Enzymes Chemicals produced by cells which help other chemical reactions to take place.

Epidemic An outbreak of a disease which affects many individuals in a population.

Extinction The dying out of the last members of a species.

Gestation Pregnancy, or the time a young mammal spends developing within its mother's womb.

Glands Groups of cells in animals or plants which produce and release a special chemical.

Immunity The ability to resist infectious diseases.

Insulation Material that does not allow heat to move across it.

Matriarch A mother that leads her family groups which may include several generations of her descendants.

Metabolic rate The rate at which chemical reactions which release energy and build tissue in living things occur.

Migration The movement from a place where conditions are unsuitable to a place where they are suitable, and back.

Nocturnal Animals that are active only during the hours of darkness.

Paganism A word used by the early Christian Church to mean religions other than Christianity, Judaism, and Islam.

Plankton Tiny animals and plants that float near the surface of the sea.

Predator An animal which catches other animals to eat.

Prehensile Able to grasp.

Sebaceous glands Glands in the skin that make sebum, an oily substance that makes hair waterproof.

Stereoscopic vision Able to see in three dimensions and so judge distances.

Umbilical cord A tube containing blood vessels that passes out of the unborn baby's navel to the placenta, where the baby's blood picks up food and oxygen from the mother's blood, and gets rid of wastes.

INDEX

Photo credits
Abbreviations: t-top, m-middle, b-bottom, r-right, l-left
Cover: Roger Vlitos; 3, 11: Kobal Collection; 22m: Polygram (Courtesy Kobal Collection); 4, 6, 7t, m, bl, 9t, 12t, 13t, b, 16-17m, 16b, 17b, 18-19m, 19t, b, 22-23, 22b, 25l, 27t, b, 28-29m, 29tl, 29mr: Frank Spooner Pictures; 5t, 8, 19m, 24: Planet Earth Pictures; 5b, 7br, 15b, 20, 23r, 25r, 29b: Mary Evans Picture Library; 9b, 10, 12-13m, 13m, 14m, 15t, m, 17t, 21t, b, 29ml: Bruce Coleman Collection; 14t: Spectrum Colour Library; 14b, 23l: Hulton Deutsch; 28b: Eye Ubiquitous; 29tr: Solution Pictures.